HumDrums

Nida Rashid

Presentation by *BookLeaf Publishing*

Web: www.bookleafpub.com

E-mail: info@bookleafpub.com

ISBN: 9789357690553

First edition 2022

To my everyday life partner, Ali.

ACKNOWLEDGEMENT

Thank you, Aisha Hakh, for thinking of me,
when you saw a poetry challenge.

True Colours

On days when
I cannot be green
When my sun shines
in smaller intervals
and vibrant
colours hidden deep within me
begin to show
When you start seeing the
bright hues
and the range of colours
I can become
in the dark
Please don't shed me
like the trees
do their leaves
I will fall
drifting further away
leaving you bare
So when the winds are rough
You must firmly believe
That my green is there

Letting Go

Silly little leaf,
Do you think I drop you
Because you've
changed colours
in the dimmer days?

Your bright colours
adorn me
They bring out
My complexity
With the sun's rays

No I let you fall only
because I know
your buds remain

If I keep you longer
you'll be browned
And I will not be able to
sustain

your beauty in the
coming cold
So I cannot keep you
Where you cannot grow

It is only because
we will meet again
when I can welcome
you with warmth
I let you go

Travels

Lifted across continents
I sat on patios
with a view
In a lovely breeze
Surrounded with tongues
That didn't speak like I do
We sought
a common humanity
in our gazes
A smile, sometimes a nod
we took delights
In common phrases

It's strange
that even in foreign lands
I look for familiarity
as safety
The sight of my flag
The excitement of someone
To talk to
I didn't realize
I missed home
When I left it
For something new

I search for familiar faces
In these new spaces
And wonder
Why I left to search
For what I left

Shield of Sadness

would rather
garner sympathy
than envy,
so advocate miseries
over bounties
When in reality
the blessings
are plenty

Is it the fear
that without
a tear
blessings
will disappear?

Or that smiles
Will be snatched
By the eyes of others
Whose attention
joy has catched

Envy is a darkness
disease in the other
And the cure is notTo dim
But
to shinebrighter

Rapid River

A stagnant river
Protests this contradiction
At the gate of the dam

Let me go,
into the rapids
Where I am free to flow

Hear my sound
Rushing, gushing
over the rocks

Let me scream
So that my slashes and splashes
Echo in the wild

Don't tame me
Like lakes and swamps
Who time turns green
And depths make blue

Let my white show
As I go rogue
And gallop
Proudly through

Plant

The barren land
begs me to plant
But I have no seeds

There's a drought of ideas
A chant of "I can't"
that gives way to the weeds

Nothing will grow
Here in the shade
I need the sun

Hoping the rays
will come to my aid
Before the day is done

Harmony

Let us
Melt into a blend of colours
That'll paint a canvas bright

Let us
Be together on sunny days
And on the darkest night

Let us
climb mountains
and reach their highest peaks

Let us
Sit still in silence
When neither of us speaks

let us be, just let us be
No longer you and I
But as a 'we'.

Sweeping the Floor

the cracks on her feet
Are more apparent to me
as she gets down on her knee
insisting on keeping the home
clean and neat
My heart pangs at a mother's gray hair
And the clank of her bangles
But she moves along
Silently determined
seemingly unaware
Muttering something about how
no one cares
she doesn't hear any
Half-hearted offer to lend a hand
she seems too occupied
in picking each
piece of dirt
every hair strand
in her housekeeping
there is no end goal
in turning
A house into a home

Watching the Garbage Men

the remains of our humanity
the evidence of our breaths
is being lugged away by two men in vests
they care not what we cast aside
do they ignore the stench of our lives
as they feed the contents of the bins
into the machine that spins
together the collective filth in a single motion
and unites each tenant into a stinky potion
these men, are they aware?
That cultures and identities are thrown in the
air?
That colour of skin matter not
As all our garbage starts to rot
All of our junk has the same fate
Even if some bags carry more weight
As our weekly remains are emptied by these
men
They allow us to begin to live again

Poetic Labour

I saw a man on the corner of the street
and thought I'd capture his struggle in a poem
his mismatched clothes,
and his cardboard-box-home
told me all I needed to know
to create an art

I've noticed him, in his moment
of watching people enter the store
he doesn't speak, but his presence
is hard to ignore
at the door
I took up my pen and paper
to understand his heart

I thought I'd cheer him up
with a rhyme or two
but what use to help him
in a way that I like to do?

He didn't need my poetry
He needed water
perhaps some food
he needed to be seen
but didn't ask to be shown

I watched him not ask
shivering in the cold,
I watched him sit looking at
each passerby
hoping to catch a
glance

I watched him suffer, so
I didn't give him a rhyme
Because he needed
To be noticed differently
I gave him my time

I took his work and asked him
What can I get you?
"Chocolate milk", he said.
So I gave him that instead.

A Bridge in a Park

Stuck on one side of the river
Someone thought of making a bridge
To make ease for people they would never see
To build a bridge is to anticipate
That another will follow the same path
and face the same hurdle

Most people have their noses
rubbing in the gravel focusing
on the pebbles and stones
But one person came with a goal
Sought a mountain on the other side
And ignored the river's flow and tide
Deciding instead to expand the world
For people unknown
Adn their compassion and forsight
In this bridge is shown

So this bride, when given attention
is not just a bridge
It is a shadow of a past hope,
Or it's just some wood nailed together
In a purposeful slope

Bravery

Run away and I come
back to the same face
There is no place in the world
to hide from
me my own fate
Any step further and I'm
met with the same realization
I cannot run from myself
Added people, added time
Collected memories
And composed a rhyme
And again and again
I return to myself
trip over my own limits
In the end it is
the company of myself
I must keep

bravery
is continuing to go on
With your own self
Knowing that in the past
it has failed
Knowing that it is not
Capable of everything

it aspires to do
Knowing that ahead
it is stuck with
it's own mistakes
And I keep going
Knowing that the self is flawed
I keep pursuing
Something bigger than the self

Bravery is committing
to my self
to be
brave enough to break it
build it
and endure it

On Worth

Did the tree ever complain
that it is not worth the rain?
Or that others, from the sun
Have more to gain?

I wonder if it thought
Some bear tastier fruit
So let them shine
I can suffer a drought
For my prickly pine

Waiting to be worthy
Is waiting for the sun
to choose where
it shines
and then holding up a shield
to stay in our darkness
complaining
it's too bright

Praying

As I stand, I surrender
here are my empty palms
I have nothing of my own
I leave behind the world
and face beyond

head low into a bow I go
giving away my reigns
as I expose my nape
acknowledging The Great

head first, I prostrate
shedding all the burdens
I carry on my shoulders
finally at rest from
dropping the weight

I pause the humming
and drumming
racing and chasing
and I sit, still
as my whispers ascend
I slowly return to the
life I know, until
the suns shifts and
I stand to surrender

Final Destination

I was gone before I left
I was here before there
Waiting but leaving
At the same time

I knew until I didn't
I was on a path that led me back
To where I started
And I stood
Confused

Where I was going, I forgot
To decide on a path
I was taught
But I couldn't figure out
Where my shoe was

When I found it on my feet
I walked to the street
That led me away from
where I thought I should go

I crossed the same road twice
ending up on the opposite side

To the place, I was standing
when I started to walk

I saw the bus with passengers
who knew where they were going
So I got in until I had to get off
pretending to have the same determination
as everyone else
who hears their stops
and descend to their destinations

Stand Still

They have raised arms and I stand in the middle
I cannot move but a little
Afraid to hurt anyone else I stand steady
Cross my arms to look stronger but I am not
ready
for the next move, because I know I cannot
stand it
If I fall all those around me will suffer
I have no pillar
No support to lean on
No one dares looks anyone in the eye
Yet everyone understands my struggle
I must endure this alone
A slight shake and everyone is moved
I can see their faces dripping
And some others are tripping
But I stand still
I let not my tension spill
I hold all the force beneath me
This is how I commute daily
on the city subway

Big City

Ode to the big city
Where dreams are
Mixed in the stenches
Of battered humanity
Where to make a dollar
They stand on the corners
Of streets
Where beggars make rhymes
 one saying,
"Give me a smile or some time,
but I'll also take a handful of dimes"
no one pauses
everyone's frowning,
busy, in a rush,
To even notice the
Toothless grin of the
Begging man who calls
them to see some
Of their own blessings
because if we saw
what we had
we'd stop the urgency
of wanting more
But no one stops
everyone is in a rush

To get somewhere
Always late
chasing time,
To fill more in their day
unsatisfied, lingering thirst
that no amount
of consumption can quench
every inch of the land
Is filled with gray
rest is found
under the
shades of tall towers
Dwarfing their dreams

Mundane

Tread through the mundane
The painting of the background
When nothing is actually seen
But everything is built
For the swiftness of action
May sweep you off your feet
If you are not first planted firmly
In the ground beneath
The building of foundation
Happens out of sight
You only see the skyscrapers
After a long, laborious fight
The white of the winter
Seems dead to the eye
If only you knew
How spring will reply

Farewell

when the sun sets
it brightens the sky
before announcing the night
there's no reason for it
to bid us farewell
so beautifully
in its oranges and pinks
I forget that it means
the coming of dark
yet when it rises
the same colours
are seen
but this time with a promise of bright
so when it sets its a reminder
that it won't be dark forever
it'll be back again tomorrow
to give some light

Bored to Board

waiting to board a flight
and no one sets up camp
in the gating area

why is no one settling in
building homes
and empires
trying to be productive
we accept their uselessness
in waiting

because it'll end
this is a temporary place
not meant for long term
we can endure boredom
for the hours it takes to
get us somewhere else

but when there is nothing more,
waiting becomes
an endless chore

no flight to board
in being bored

Hum Drums

Amidst the hum drums
There comes a new tone
That takes us out of the known
We call that life and try to contain
It before it slips by
a picture captures a moment in time
it is the desperate want to remain
in that memory forever
even while living in it now
It is to think of a day without
this exact feeling
already anticipating the lack
Of the people here to experience it
It sends it forward
It tries to hold it while it lasts
to preserve it for later
to look back and say
oh that good old day
but a poem doesn't live in the moment
it seeks forever in the now
it knows that what is in front
won't disappear
it will be repeated in another's life
perhaps another time
there is forever in that moment

not fleeting by, but captured
To be relieved in exact sentiment
As long as it is read